When your old thoughts aren't working, try some NEW Thoughts To Think

Inspiration, Mind Nudges and Mental Strategy

Written and Illustrated by
Heather Frey

Copyright 2020 Heather Frey

ALL RIGHTS RESERVED. This book contains material protected under International and Federal Copyright Laws and Treaties. Any unauthorized reprint or use of this material is prohibited. No part of this book may be reproduced or transmitted in any form or by any means, electronic or mechanical, including photocopying, recording, or by any information storage and retrieval system without express written permission from the author/publisher.

ISBN: 978-1-64184-521-2 (Paperback)

For my beautiful girls -
You are my heart and soul. You helped me laugh during a time when I didn't think I could even smile. You are both pure brilliance.
To my wonderful husband -
Your patience, support and love let me go through everything I needed to go through to get "here".
And for my sister -
I would not be the person I am without you.

Introduction

It's not easy to completely change how you think but you can shift your perspective. Life shifts comes from attitude shifts. You can decide whether you let yourself get riled up, or you let it go; you can decide whether you stay mad or you don't; and you can decide if you let one opinion ruin your goal or not.

I'm always inspired by those amazing survivor stories about people who have overcome devastating injuries and illness, or horrible life experiences. Despite what's happened to them, you see them back at life, winning races, getting married, going to school, lifting tons of weight, getting degrees, pursuing their dreams... they go on in spite of what was, or still is, against them. And we are all in awe of their perseverance and courage and wonder, how do they do that?! With one thing.. supreme master of attitude. Truth is, I'm in awe of anyone who sets goals and makes them happen because I know (as I'm sure you do too), that the road to that goal wasn't smooth.

But they shifted their brains to focus on the right things, the things that bring them solutions which bring them accomplishments and in turn rewards them with joy, calm, and happiness. They realize (or have always known), life is too short to muck it up with other people's "muck", even our own.

    I've been through some tough things in my life, most of us have, and for awhile, I thought, "this is it. I'll never be happy again. I'll pretend happy and fake smile, but I'm broken now." But when I looked down at the faces of my beautiful little girls I realized, that's not ok. That's not good enough for them and it's not good enough for me, after all I have to live in this brain. They deserve better, and I deserve better. I had to realize that I deserved to be happy and needed to show them how to do it, even when things don't work out. I needed to show them that just because you lose doesn't mean it's over. I needed them to see that it's ok to fall, fail and be sad, but you brush yourself off and keep going until it gets better. And it will… if you keep going. I needed to show them that life is wavy, filled with up swings and down turns, it's not a straight line of happiness. Struggle is normal. It doesn't feel good, and sometimes it just plain hurts, but it helps us learn what we need to know. It teaches us what's important and what is not, and it builds the strength and character we need to kick butt in this life. My goal was/is to be one of those survivors, even if I'm the only one who knows it.

So I hope these "Thoughts To Think" help you reconsider where you are in your life, what you're capable of, and that you have the power to create whatever you want to create by merely moving out a defeating thought and replacing it with a defiant one. More often than not, we're the only ones in our way, doubting ourselves, not giving ourselves enough credit, fear of failure, and the hits go on and on. But what if you could clear your mind-slate of all the defeating chatter? It's amazing how you can change an outcome from negative to positive with a simple shift of thought or reaction.

You literally get to steer your life in the direction you want to go based on nothing more than your thoughts. Easier said than done? Sometimes. But maybe, sometimes, it's easier than you think.

If you want to change
who you are
you have to change how
you talk to yourself.

*Wake up
from everyday routine.
Wake up
and realize you can do
and have more.
Wake up
and do what you
set out to do.
Wake up
and smell the coffee.*

Cotton balls were used to make the steam, tinfoil for the sun and the cup was formed with sturdy watercolor paper.

Life has a way of burying dreams.
As children, we know exactly what we want to be when we grow up and there is no fear that it won't or can't happen, it is simply so. But time begins to cover us with doubt and responsibility until we forget those dreams.
But they're still there.
Life can bury your heart. It's up to you to grab a shovel and start digging.

You're not born with confidence, it's something you gain every time you throw yourself over an obstacle.

A goal isn't a thing,
it's a series of action steps
to get you there.
Your biggest goal starts
with just one little step.

Be accountable.
Blaming gives away too much of your power.

Being positive doesn't mean you have to be in a good mood all the time. Sometimes being positive means getting **mad** - mad enough to get yourself moving, and mad enough to finally make the positive changes you need. Get mad enough to get motivated.

You are who you think
you are so
if you change your mind,
you change who you
think you are.

Doubt is normal but feeding it will eventually swallow up all your drive, enthusiasm and creativity until you're left with nothing but anger. When doubt rolls in, just let it roll right out. Don't let it live there.

Stop waiting for someone
to save you…
you ARE that person.

Stop taking everything so personally. When you are immune to the opinions and actions of others, their negativity can have no influence on your life.
Other people's opinions are about their own reality not yours.
So pick your battles and let the rest just roll off your back.

I used marbles, beads and watercolor paper for the background. The marbles have many different meanings.

You can't change it so don't let it change you.

Look around.
Notice the dishes next to your computer
because you have enough to eat.
Notice your sneakers on the floor
because you're healthy enough to move.
Notice the laughter of your children
because they are happy.
Notice your boss who just walked by
because you are employed.
Notice all the calls you need to return
because you have friends.
Notice the lists with 100 things to do
because you have a full life.
Notice the messages and conversations
because people love you.
Notice all the goodness around you right this
minute.. stop what you're doing right now and
really look around you.
Life brightens when you begin to truly **see**
all the things you have, not all the things you
don't. What you take for granted is someone
else's dream.

Don't let the sadness of the world suck you under or you just become more of the sadness. Protect your light, with everything you've got, so you can use it to light up the darkness.

Replace worry
with strategy.

Remember when you were a kid and anything was possible? That hasn't changed.

The minute you start worrying about what everyone else is doing is the minute you start to lose your own path.

There is always another way.
Just because you don't have the answers
doesn't mean there isn't one.
Reach for…
seek…
listen…
ask…
and never give up on finding
your answers.

They're there.

Priorities aren't something you can waffle on. They must have a no-matter-what commitment otherwise don't be surprised by your *sorta results* from your *kinda effort*.

Don't take your life for granted for
one more minute.
Don't for one more minute
waste your time with
worry and regret.
Don't for one minute hold yourself back
from your happiness.
Don't for one minute believe you don't
deserve happiness.
Don't for one minute think this minute
doesn't count.

BE BOLD

or someone will bold all over you.

Every day you don't do what you set out to do is one less day to be who you want to become.

Stop worrying about what other people think. People are resistant to change, whether it be our own, or that of friends and family. But if you're going to move yourself UP through life, you're going to have to make yourself immune to most of the opinions and advice of others. People generally mean well, some don't, so filter out the "noise" and trust yourself. Your success has to be paved by you, and you alone, and what other people think is none of your business.

Don't hesitate.
Regrets create scars
on your soul.

Ever notice that when you're in a bad mood and one of your favorite songs comes on, your mood is instantly transformed to happiness? Apply this to your life. When you stop thinking about what's bothering you,
you stop being upset.
Pick your battles.
Some things just aren't worth thinking about and dwelling on. Turn the station and live your *favorite song*.

Don't share your dreams with just anyone or you may not get the response you want. Talking with too many people about your plans opens you up to their opinions and agendas and you often get a response that pertains to *them* not you.
Protect your dreams, they're too important to share with just anyone.

Success isn't the sum of your victories, it's the sum of your efforts.

Be careful how you talk to yourself.
Your soul is listening.

In order to get ahead you're going to have to GIVE UP.
Give up defeating thoughts and dialogues.
Give up the notion that *this is all there is*.
Give up bad habits that work against you.
Give up some familiar and comfortable.
Give up people who don't cheer you on.
Give up the idea that you are any less magnificent and capable than anyone else.

Belief -
You don't have to know 100% that it will work, you just have to know that if you give it 100% it could.

Life isn't against you. It's just pushing on you to see how hard you'll push back.

You are a magnet.
Every positive and negative action you make, from the smallest to the biggest, creates a ripple of energy into the universe that will either pull things towards you or push them away.

Reaching out to a friend, helping a stranger, being a good listener... these are the kinds of ripples that pull towards you the people and situations you need to achieve your goals and create the life you dream of.

But it works in the opposite direction as well. Anger and resentment don't just stay inside your head, they play out in your life and repel the people and things that are most important so you have to let it go or you'll just attract more of it to you.

You are a magnet.

Choose what you want to attract.

If you only knew
how powerful
you really are,
you wouldn't
be afraid to try.

Holding on may feel secure but you can't fly if you don't LET GO.

Your day is filled with thousands of decisions, each one branching off to a whole new series of decisions. But when it comes to the big stuff, the most impactful decisions are the ones you don't make at all.

Indecision keeps you stuck and stunted in the middle of **what is** and **what could be**. Make a decision.

Because even the wrong choice gets you moving towards the right one.
Deciding is the kick-start to motion,
which turns into action, and it's **action** that takes you where you want to go.

You can't change what happened but you can decide if you use it to light you up,
or burn you down.

Power isn't something that's given to you, it's something you already have.

YES and NO.
Simple, yet powerful, life-changing words.
Grab your power by picking the right one.
Say NO to:
- doing things you don't want to do
- hanging with life-sucking people
- doing things that go against your gut
- filling your day with everything but you

Say YES to:
- new challenges
- having more fun
- taking a risk
- being a goof
- trading fear for excitement
- all that is soul-filling

You are powerful beyond measure.
You have the power to change your life with the switch of a thought.

You are stronger than you know.

What would you be doing if there was nothing to hold you back?
Then go do THAT.

Nothing is holding you back but you.

Don't wait for someone else to do it.
Or fix it,
or take care of it,
or get it right,
or give you a break,
or make you happy,
or finish it.
YOU do it.
Don't leave something as important as *it* -
your life - in the hands of someone else. No
one will ever care about ***it*** more than you.

You're done!
You've had enough!
It's just not working.
Or is it?
You have to give it enough time to work. Whether you're talking about your body goals or life goals, strategy needs time to gain momentum.

No one is without fear.
No one is
without struggle.
But it's those that refuse
to live in it that can find
true joy, and joy is what
battles fear and struggle.

Don't try to change them.
Change your
reaction to them.

There is a life force to kindness that doesn't stop when you walk away, it permeates into all the people you touch, and in turn, all the people they touch. And that kindness gets shared and passed around until your one act of kindness can multiply into a wave of generosity and compassion.

Be as kind as you can whenever you can, even to those you think don't quite deserve it because you never know if someone is going through a rough time and your one simple gesture can lift their day.

Kindness has power… for the person you're giving it to, and for you.

There is only a fight
if you engage with it.
There is only anger
if you spin about it.
There is only fear
if you worry about it.
Nothing resides in you
unless you let it.

Are you listening?
Are you paying attention to all the good stuff they're saying to you and about you?
Quit dismissing the compliments and praise. Funny how you'll dismiss the 10 really great things people say to you but only hear that one not-so-great thing, or the nagging voice of doubt in your head.
Stop it.
LISTEN to the compliments. Take heart in the fact that most don't need to say anything but they do. People are simply reflecting back the greatness in you. They see how hard you work, and the passion you put into everything you do. And you're suppose to hear it so that you finally start *believing* it.

You are limitless.
When you believe this,
you will live the life you
are meant to live.

LOVE

It's one of the most powerful
life tools you have.
It moves you forward,
connects you,
heals what hurts,
relieves what aches
restores faith
repairs what's broken
and softens the blows
that life sometimes throws.
Give it, receive it, and always hold onto it.
It's the only true magic in this world.

You are equipped.
You have everything you need.
You're smart, resourceful, hard working, and capable. Not a tool is missing.
The only thing you need to do is toss your fear of trying. Once you do, you can add one of your most important tools....confidence.

When you stop thinking
about what's
in your way…
there's nothing in
your way.

You're playing it over and
over in your head
but it always ends the
same way.
Shake it off.
Stop rolling around in it,
and step over it.

Like storms on a ship or turbulence in a plane, one minute life is fine, the next, it's all over the place and you're gripped with worry. But remember, storms pass, turbulence settles and smoother air is ahead. Turbulence is just part of this ride but the calmer you stay through it all, the quicker it passes behind you, and it always does.

Everyone struggles. Everyone has pain. Everyone has battle scars and war wounds, and everyone is just trying to put their pieces together the best they can. So as you move about your day, treat people with a little more kindness, a little more patience, and a little more understanding.

Treat people as if they had *your struggles*.

You deserve the life your heart is telling you to live. There is no justifying living an unhappy life.

If you give so much
to everyone
but yourself,
you'll have
nothing left to give
which defeats the purpose
of giving.

Don't "poor me" yourself out of your power.

You've had some tough breaks and you've been through trauma but if you want a happy life, you have to stop blaming those things for not being where you want to be.

You are strong! Look at everything you've gone through and survived.

Close those painful chapters,

don't let them be an excuse to live an unfulfilled life. You pushed through the bad stuff, you can certainly push through to get to the good stuff.

Quit trying to be perfect.
The mental energy it takes to beat yourself up for not being something that doesn't even exist is exhausting. Tearing yourself down doesn't make you better, it makes you worse and chips away at the very heart of what makes you, *you*.

It's great to want to improve and expand your life, but do that from a place of loving yourself not hating yourself. Instead of "perfect" be - spirited, quirky, weird, creative, passionate, unusual, out of the ordinary. Aren't these usually the most fun and interesting
people anyway?

There is NO perfect. You are a fluid being, moving in and out of knowing and not knowing which is exactly how it's suppose to be. That's called **learning**. And as you move through these states of being (and 100 phases in between), you'll make mistakes because that is the cost of being human.

Let go of perfection, what truly makes someone "perfect" is their ability to see their imperfections as what makes them beautiful. Embrace your cool, unique way of seeing and navigating the world.

If you can't say anything nice to yourself,
don't say anything at all.

The only way they can
take your power
is if you let them.

Some parts of life should simply be ignored. Not everything needs to be reacted to or considered.

If you let all life's annoyances and critical people into your brain space, not only will it waste your time, but it eventually sucks the creative and peaceful life right out of you. Ignore most of it.

Don't let their negative swallow your positive.

KEEP GOING.
Your swinging confidence feels like you're at the playground... uncertainty loves to play mind games.
But feeling uncertain does not change your **facts**.
- It does NOT change what you've accomplished;
- it does NOT change what you're good at,
- it does NOT change your limitless potential, and
- it does NOT change who you are.
  Keep going. The world need you.
It might feel like you're swinging backwards but it's only a matter of time before your swing comes screaming forward.

Negativity stunts your growth.

Don't be afraid to shine.
The world needs as much light as possible.
Light brings clarity and warmth both figuratively and literally, so the more you shine, the more of your road you'll be able to see. And in your process, your shine will light the path for others.

Shine your light.
You're the only one who
has the dimmer.

Without focus and action,
you're just
hoping for the best.

We have a tendency to go about our daily lives in autopilot only half paying attention, but not paying attention means you're not correcting and adjusting to the needs and demands of your life's goal. Autopilot keeps you safe, but you'll end up flying in circles never really getting where you want to go. Pay attention.
I mean, really pay attention.. to all the beautiful pieces of your life because it's those pieces that will bring you peace.

    Take the controls. Whatever your goals, if you don't focus on what you're doing and **why**, you'll end up flying the same pattern over and over. Make a flight plan, set the course, and take control.

Bask in your gratefuls.
There will always be something to grumble about, someone who wronged you, something that didn't work out,
but if you live in that mindset, trying to move forward is like trying to walk through knee-deep mud.
   But if you live with the attitude of seeing all you *have* — family and friends who love you, enough food to eat, accomplishments to be proud of, opportunities to come…
then the bright glow of your gratitude will burn off the haze of what you think you don't have.

Our greatest joys are
not just in our
own achievements but in
helping others
reach theirs.

You crave peace
but you hang onto
the things that
won't let you have it…

IT'S TIME TO LET GO.

You don't have to play the hand you were given. You can swap out cards, get some new ones, even start a new game. Because as much as "cards" - life - is a game of chance, it's also a game of strategy, and you can control your strategy. You were given a whole deck with endless ways to play and limitless ways to win. You many not get to choose the cards you were dealt, but you can decide on the limitless ways to play them.

Don't second guess yourself into doubt.
You ARE headed in the right direction and you ARE doing the right things.
Every detail may not work out, but the big picture will, unless you let your doubt do the steering. You wouldn't have made it this far if you weren't on the right road.

Falling down doesn't mean losing.
It's conditioning for GETTING UP.

It seems like life is either
coming apart
or coming together.
It's a fragile balance and
sometimes changes daily.
But no matter which way
things are falling, as long as
you protect and cherish the
most important
things in life
- health, family, friends -
you can weather anything.

Yes, those are real egg shells saved from breakfast. The mosaic is made from the egg carton.

Leaders don't wait for opportunities,
they create them.

Extract the emotion from what needs to
get done and just get it done.
Stop worrying about it,
stop over-thinking it, and
stop procrastinating it.
None of those things make it better, it just
keeps you stuck and stalled in that one spot.
Get strong with yourself, leave emotion out of
it, and go get YOU done.

You are absolutely ok
just the way you are.
Don't let anyone convince
you otherwise,
not even you.

Stop trying to keep up with everyone else. It's an impossible pace to sustain and steals time and energy away from creating the unique *you* you're suppose to become.
Who you want to be has nothing to do with anyone else so don't waste your time feeling you need to run in anyone else's race.
In fact, if you view your life as a race, you'll run right by it and miss the amazing details of your story. Don't try to keep up, run, skip, walk, weave, jog your own course.

Align yourself with greatness.
Filter out what doesn't work, discard the garbage that doesn't belong in your brain, and remove people who suck the life and motivation out of you. Get supremely clear about your goals and surround yourself with only those that lift you, encourage you, inspire you, and laugh with you.
Align and focus because greatness attracts more greatness.

When you create what
you want
you attract what
you need.

You'll never get what you want if you don't believe you deserve it. If you don't believe in your value then how can anyone else? Confidence in yourself attracts people's confidence in you.

Give up your need for approval.

You don't need permission to live your dreams.

So you
fell down.
So what.
Success
comes
with more
downs
than ups.
Your road
is a narrow
path so
you're
going to
fall.

The sooner you accept that disappointment is part of the journey, the less time you'll spend being disappointed and the faster you'll be at getting up.

Strength
is in the way
you carry your
circumstance.

Always focus on the outcome you WANT. Adjust your strategy not your dreams.

This isn't it.
This isn't all there is.
Even though things feel like they're not moving, they are. There are invisible forces making sure things are in place for your shift. Keep pushing forward, making sure to do what you need to do, but be patient.
You can't hurry a process.

Mean thoughts, and constant complaining doesn't change one thing except
your own brain.
Speak negative and you receive negative.
Think negative, and you create negative.
Either way, it doesn't do anything but push away the things you want, and the people you love.

   And the negativity doesn't just stay in your head, it oozes out in your tone of voice, your body language, and the way you deal
with people.
And they feel it.
Be careful with your words… and thoughts.
What we say and do, and the attitude with which we say and do it, can make a situation right or send it where it was never
meant to go.

You get out of life the attitude you put into it.

Being grateful isn't just an act of thinking, its an act of doing. It doesn't take much - a harder hug, a phone call, a smile. It is the *action of gratitude* which releases energy that can be transferred from one person to another to another. And the beauty is, the more gratitude you give, the more gratitude you **gain**, and the more gratitude you gain, the more you have to give.

Be gracious.
Be kind.
Be helpful.
Be supportive.
Be forgiving.
Creating good energy
deflects bad energy.

Stop thinking so hard and just do it. Sometimes it IS just that simple.

Great things are coming.
But you have to believe you're worthy or else you won't be able to see them.
Self doubt and damaged confidence are life-blockers and sabotagers and can blind you to what's right in front of you.
You deserve it.
Believe it.
Grab it and
RUN with it!

One of the best decisions
you can make,
is to simply
make a decision.

Let them be.
Requiring that they behave a certain way for your acceptance stunts their growth, as well as yours. Everyone has to find their own way and sometimes stepping into mistakes are the lessons they (we) need so they avoid making them again. You don't have to like everything, but accept who they are, as you want them to accept who you are.

Why is it that you value the things you're not good at and discount the things *you are good at*?

Why do you think they're so great because they can do "that" but you're not so great even though you can do "this"?
Don't dismiss your gifts.

The fact that it comes easily to you doesn't make it less valuable, if anything, it makes it more. The things you're good at were put inside you to move you up and move you forward and to help others do the same. Relish your gifts. They were given to you for a reason.

Do it yourself.
Don't expect anyone
to grasp the
supreme importance
of your dreams.

You are exactly where you believe you are. If you think you're behind in your life's plan, under your problems, and unaccomplished in your goals, then you are.

But if you think - problems are part of life and are as big or small as I decide they are; that life rolls out in its own time, not mine; and that if I truly look at what I've accomplished I'm much farther ahead than I give myself credit for - then THAT is true.

One truth keeps you sad and frustrated and one truth keeps you moving forward.

Pick.

You have to raise your hand or life might not see you.

Every day you emit vibrations.
It's in the subtle way you speak to a cashier and the obvious ways you love your children.
It's in the impatience with your coworkers and the understanding you give your friends.
It's in the quiet way you help a stranger and the loud way you laugh with your friends.
With each of these vibrations you send a pulse into the universe that reacts with consequence.
Be aware of your vibrations and only send out what you want to get back.

Standing in the
same spot,
you can look down
and see nothing but dirt
and concrete
or
look up
and see the sun and
infinite sky.
You choose your view.

Make it you.
Make it you who turns the mood.
Make it you who turns the situation.
Make it you who finds the solution.
Make it you who shifts things back
in right direction.
Make it you who uses your power for good.
You may not want it to be you, but it won't
get better without you.

When people live a life seeing only the negative, they have a hard time seeing anything else. There's no point to living in what's wrong unless your mission is to fix it.

Filter it.
Don't let it get to you.
Don't let them get to you.
And don't let the situation get to you.
If you do, you lose your power, your focus, and your momentum. Get laser sharp with your goal and only let in the things that lift you and the people who support you. Everything else should be filtered.

Your limits are set
by you,
not anyone else.

Start being proud
of yourself.
Appreciate the beauty in
you, and accept what
you want to change
as a challenge
not a flaw.

There is no reward for suffering and no medal for working so hard you're about to fall apart.

Step away for a bit and feed yourself. You need both physical and emotional nourishment.

Go for a drive, a walk, a run, to the gym, to a favorite store, call a friend.. whatever reenergizes you and helps to feed your passion and motivation.

Give yourself a break.

Nothing can keep going without fuel

... not even you.

Leave your mental fence.
You put it up
but you can
tear it down.
Your best life is on the
other side.

We all have damage.
Every single one of us has gone through something difficult or traumatic that has changed us. Sometimes the damage is so deep, we're not sure we can get back to who we were.

And you may not be able to, and that's ok because sometimes things are torn down so they can be rebuilt stronger and even more beautiful. Perfection doesn't create beauty, it's the imperfections and stories of strength and perseverance that make something truly awe inspiring.

You have your foundation - your heart - and with that, you can reinvent and renovate any way you like. Too hard? You've made it through the worst part..the tearing down part, rebuilding is the exciting and exhilarating part. On the other side of your renovations lie confidence and peace and a story of strength that will inspire others.

What are you waiting for, everything to be perfect? For things to get better?
GO NOW.
…because there will never be a perfect time. Isn't the point of making it happen, to make things better? But how will things get better if you're always *waiting* for them to get better? Go now.

OVER thinking
leads to
UNDER doing.

The beaten path is worn out.
You can try it, but it's crowded with everyone doing the same thing.
Don't be afraid to do your own thing your own way. The innovators didn't do what everyone else did, they invented what everyone is doing.

Don't let guilt consume you. Let go of it, solve it, fix it, apologize for it, but don't let it steal your life, or your light.

Don't let them change you.
Don't let their opinions and unhappiness seep into your soul. Their negativity has to do with their own issues, not yours.
If it's someone you can filter, do it.
Life is hard enough without having people judge you and pull you down. If it's not someone you can't filter, filter what you tell them. **Not everybody deserves the honor or your energy.**

Be grateful for your fear.
Let it move you to
your solution.

Be still.
Stop moving all the time.
You think hurrying to get it all done it will create more time, but it just robs you of it. Constant busyness and over-hurrying blinds you to your actual life happening right in front of your eyes. You'll miss opportunities you're suppose to see, people who love you, and your children who just want you to be still long enough to really be with them.
You don't have to be busy all the time.
Your value isn't in how much you do, it's *what* you do.

Whatever you think is holding you back is only holding you back because you think it is.

You are beautiful.
We believe it when we're children,
that we are a beautiful princess or
the strong hero. But somewhere
along the line, we lose that ability
to see ourselves in a positive light.
Don't forget, you are STILL that
child and your dreams matter just
as much today as they did then.

To just BE is true beauty.

-Heather Frey

Don't let them steal your energy.
Those that don't have enough will grab onto you and try to suck yours out. Some just steal it for the thrill of it.
Shields UP!
Protect your precious energy, and only put it into the things that light you up and the people who share theirs with you.

Standing up to them is when you find out who you are.

Where did you get the idea that you were suppose to get it all done, every day, all the time, and keep a smile on your face?

Why have you bought into the fake notion that everyone else has it together except you?

And why do you continue to zero in on your flaws and ignore the magnificent things you do every day?

Nobody has it all together all the time. NOBODY.

If you're lucky you'll have a good streak where things run smoothly and everything falls into place, but then chaos will strike again, it always does. It's **normal** so leave yourself alone. Be nice to you and find the humor instead of being hard on yourself. Just do the best you can, even if your best on that day is to do nothing at all.

It's a long ride so you can either throw your hands up and say WHEEE! or grip the seat in terror. You'll get there either way.

Get grateful.
If you're having a hard time finding it,
grab your perspective as well.
As you shop for too many things,
some can't provide for their children.
As you stress about deadlines,
some are looking for a job.
As you spend money eating out,
some can't buy food.
And as you drive from place to place,
some lay in bed battling illness.
Keep your life in perspective. Staying grounded and grateful are your best tools for finding your piece of *peace*.

ACT like you can, until you can.

belief will catch up later

What are you waiting for?
If you're waiting for a green light, it's been green since you were born.
Put your foot on your gas, and GO.
There will be slow-downs, construction, detours, even closed roads, but there's always a way around. There's nothing in your way except your own mental roadblocks and you have the power to move those out of your way… *this very minute.*

Letting go doesn't mean
you stop trying,
it means you TRUST that
the efforts and energy
you're putting in is
enough to get you there.

Keep Your COOL

"Losing it" never gets you anywhere except in trouble or embarrassed. Calm down and chill out because keeping your cool always gives you the upper hand.

The sun and heat waves are made from the match stick heads and with the leftover sticks I created the waves. Her hair is made from painted watercolor paper cut into thin strips.

For better or worse, if you don't give it your attention, it will die.

If you don't give your time and energy to the the things you love and the people you cherish, they can't grow and thrive, and they will eventually disappear.

The good news is that this works in the opposite direction as well.

When you don't give your time and energy to the negative forces in your life, you starve them of their power over you and eventually they die and disappear.

Give attention- or starve attention-
Choose wisely.

Don't let your head hold back your heart.

Stand up for yourself.
No one will know how
strong you are if you're
always sitting…
including you.

You don't need to filter what you think through anyone. You don't need to run it by them, get their take on it, see what they think, and most especially, you don't need to get their approval.
Trust yourself.
Take in a few trusted opinions but keep the rest out. Asking too many people what *they* think only stifles what *you* think.

When you create

what you want,

you attract

what you need.

You don't recognize yourself.
The confidence and motivation you used to have has been covered by responsibility and your multiplying roles as mother, father, spouse, caretaker, bread winner, and the list goes on. There doesn't seem to be much time anymore to just rest, let alone tackle your dreams.
But you have to, and it's time.
It's pulling at you so no more putting it off and no more putting yourself at the end of the line… it's time to find you and BE you.
No, it's not selfish to step to the front, especially when you've been letting everyone cut in front of you for so long.
How can you take care of everything and everyone else if you're resentful, depleted and exhausted?
The fact is, the best gift you can give the people you love is your happiest and strongest self… and then show them how they can get there too.

Don't waste your time saying yes to things you don't want to do. Don't *yes* yourself out of a happy life.

You want it NOW because now seems like the best time to have it, but when you look back at so many things you wanted "now", you can see why it was a good thing you didn't get them. The process of waiting is the process of learning the lessons you'll need to conquer success and have the wisdom to keep it.

Stick with it and when the time is right, you'll get it ***now.***

We walk in a daze, taking for granted the life we have been given. We get so caught up in routine and tasks that we walk right by the beauty in every day. Time is fleeting - don't forget to pay attention.

I cut up a calendar using the months for the trunk, the weeks are the branches and the days are the leaves. I also used bark from a tree.

Don't try to convince people you're worthy.
Don't work at being appreciated.
Don't waste time trying to prove yourself.
Instead-
work on letting go of your need to please,
work on letting yourself just **be,**
and work on allowing yourself to shine.

**Do these things and
appreciation will *APPEAR.***

Flaws don't make
you weak,
thinking you're weak
makes you weak.

Life is a juggle.

Of course you know this because you're doing it right now - you're juggling 50 open tabs on your computer, 13 projects you're half-way through, adding to the list of calls you need to make, and feeling bad you forgot to return a client's email, etc, etc. If you thrive on this, more power to you.

But if you don't, you're cheating yourself. You have so many balls in the air that more often than not, you end up dropping all of them so you never (rarely) end up completing what you set out to do because you're constantly chasing after the dropped balls.

Pick one thing to complete and finish it all the way through. Then move to the next...the key is, finish *one thing at a time*.

Yes, you have a lot to do, and lots of dreams to conquer but you have to put down some of those balls so you can finally stop *chasing* what you want and actually get it.

You get what you give.
So if you're not getting
what you want,
ask yourself if you're
giving what you want.

Find your center.
Life is like walking on a beam, balancing what works and doesn't work, while trying to stay above conflict and problems.
But you will fall.
You have to fall.
Because every time you're thrown off balance, you climb back up and learn how to correct and regain control, and most importantly, you learn how to avoid getting thrown off balance in the first place.
Part of finding stability is finding what throws you off balance.

Not everything needs to be considered or reacted to. Hate, negativity, and pettiness, comes from sad people who only want to suck you down with them. Don't get sucked, rise above it, dismiss it, and ignore it.

Let nothing steal your joy.
You will let things roll off your back.
You will accept you don't have control.
You will be ok with not always being right.
You will find the humor and lessons
when things don't work out.
And you'll stop expecting others
to be different
because YOU will be the difference.
Take back your joy,
and then let it spill over onto everyone else
so they can find theirs.

Flip your switch, pull the trigger, let it go....
don't let what you think is possible hold you back from what IS possible.

Trust it will work out.

You followed your heart, listened to your gut, and made every step for a reason.
Each attempt has had a purpose, and each attempt has brought you closer to your goal even if it doesn't feel that way right now.

Trust yourself.

Make a clear mind your super power.

Slow.
Down.

Not in living life but in actually seeing it.

You can watch it with your head hanging out of a moving car, whizzing by

OR

you can stop at the rest areas, hike a trail, get a little lost, nap by the lake, and take in your amazing view.

Don't be so anxious to get there, that you miss the magnificent scenery of your life.

Do you see yourself as a victim
or a fighter?

Is yours a story of tragedy
or survival?

Do you feel you never have enough
or you have everything you need?

Do you think you're unlucky because of what hasn't happened or
lucky for everything that has?

Life is hard. No denying it. But when we frame our thoughts and views to magnify what's right and good it helps minimize what's wrong.
 It might take some practice but when things start to get bumpy, stop the negative dialogue and instead -
reflect on the beauty that surrounds you, appreciate how far you've come, remember the lessons which have brought you wisdom, and most importantly, treasure the people who you love and are there for you.

When you change how you look at your situation, you change your situation.

Circumstances can
create barriers,
but your
power is far greater
then what is
standing in front of you.

The brain

You've rolled it over and over and you still can't decide or figure it out. Then shut it down and give your brain a rest. Sometimes when you simply *stop thinking*, the answers come all by themselves. Notice how some of your best ideas come when you're not thinking about anything at all?

It's hard to know what's happening in the game when you're getting roughed up in the middle of it so just step away, grab a seat on the sidelines for a bit and just watch and observe. It's so much easier to gain perspective and see how to restrategize when you step back. Now get back in there!

Stop or keep going?
If stopping will bring you peace, then do it. But if stopping is a way to avoid what's hard, you'll be sorry. Stopping for the wrong reasons will only bring more pain and frustration. The only way to a fulfilled life and a peaceful mind is to give your
dreams everything you've got and then
give some more.
Yes it's hard, but regret is so much harder.

Asking for help doesn't
make you weak,
it makes you
STRONG.

Where will you drive your day? Will you let the small things get to you or will you let them stay small? The smaller you see life's annoyances, the bigger your life will be.

The world gets your vibe.
Nobody will treat you differently until
you treat yourself differently.
You won't get respect until
you respect yourself.

The world doesn't respond to what we want,
it responds to how we *act* and what we *do*.

Change how you speak to yourself and
others will too.
Change what you will put up with and you
won't have to put up with it anymore.
Change your vibe, and you change your life.

Defeat
is a frame
of mind not
a state of
being.

Don't personalize failure. It's just another word for "try it again a different way."

Pulling this book together was me overcoming so many of the things I've written about here so if even a few of my thoughts resonate with you and help you change your "view", I would consider it a success.

You have it in you. There is so so much left for you to do. Don't waste one more minute being mean to yourself, it solves nothing, you'll only block your magnificence waiting to come out. **Go, be amazing!**

www.ingramcontent.com/pod-product-compliance
Lightning Source LLC
Chambersburg PA
CBHW071346080526
44587CB00017B/2986